MIRACLE IN THE MARKETPLACE

*Healing and Loving
in the Modern World*

Henry Libersat

Resurrection Press
Mineola, NY

Nihil obstat: Monsignor James Amos, Vicar General
              Diocese of Pensacola-Tallahassee
              May 22, 1990

Imprimatur: Most Rev. J. Keith Symons
              Bishop of Pensacola-Tallahassee
              May 22, 1990

First published in 1990 by   Resurrection Press, Ltd.
                          P.O. Box 248
                          Williston Park, NY 11596

ISBN 1-878718-03-7
Library of Congress Catalog Number 90-070772

Cover Design: John Murello

Printed in the United States of America by Faith Printing.

To Bishop Thomas J. Grady,
second Bishop of Orlando,
in gratitude for his pastoral leadership
and vision for lay ministry
and for the gift of my ordination
to the permanent diaconate.

Contents

PART I
The Catholic Laity—A Personal Agenda

PART II
Called and Chosen—A People Set Apart

PART III
The Challenge:
You Give Them to Eat

Foreword

The one word that is used with frequency in the Church that sets my teeth on edge is the word—laity. Granted it has a place but it should be used sparingly, if at all. Although I've never discussed this with Henry Libersat, I believe he would be very sympathetic with my abhorrence for the term because of what these pages contain.

Within the first few pages, the reader will be able to sense the zeal or, better, fire in the guts of the writer for his subject. He is surely not guilty of dichotomizing the laity from the clergy. Nor is he willing to allow the marketplace to function according to its own laws which are, for the most part, economic.

Henry Libersat has a really concrete way of moving people beyond a personal, private agenda into being people who are concerned with pursuing Christ's agenda. He does this with a modicum of theory and a large dose of practical suggestions. Underlying his suggestions is a firm conviction that each person is empowered by baptism to be "for others" and to give them the bread they need that lasts unto eternal life.

What is most satisfying about the conceptions and reflections of this deacon of the Diocese of Orlando is their non-churchiness. He is convinced, as is the official Church itself, that the special role of the Christian is in the temporal order, in the life of the world, within its structures, professions and institutions.

The need for such an emphasis and, therefore, for a work such as this is evident in some of the statistics he gives. These were compiled by David C. Leege and can be found in Report #11 of the Notre Dame Study of Catholic Parish Life. According to that study, almost 51% of the Church-going Catholics responding to this survey "participate in no parish activities besides Mass and devotions." And even more disconcerting "nearly 57% do not participate in any civic activities."

But this kind of data must be interpreted carefully since the impression is easily conveyed that holiness happens when we are involved in extracurricular soirees, so to speak, rather than going about our ordinary rounds, our usual tasks, our regular responsibilities. One of the keys to developing a secular holiness, to growing in union with God in the world, is the regular experiencing of God in one's everyday work and relationships. One does not have to do the work of supererogation as we used to call it—the heroic, out of the ordinary feat—to find God or win God's favor. To expect to find the "saints" only where people are doing something out of the ordinary either politically or in some parish activity misses the point of the book and the point of the Church's stress on where the unique vocation of the Christian plays itself out, namely, in the world.

In thinking this through, one of the helpful distinctions made by the author is between the Church and the Kingdom of God. If the work of the Church were simply identified with building the Church, then the measure of our holiness and goodness would be in proportion to the work one does for the Church or the number of one's Church activities. But if Christ is after bigger game, and he is, then the transformation of the world is the name of that game. But the world, transformed through and in Christ, is the Kingdom of God.

The gist of what the author is saying with such concreteness here is that this transformation doesn't take place from the sky but through the cleansed hands and dancing feet and trained minds and focused hearts that have come to know the Lord. People, in a word, are the instruments of God for bringing about God's Kingdom or the new heavens and the new earth, as I would prefer to call it.

Libersat speaks candidly and, therefore, with authority on the subject of prayer. He has personally learned that a life without prayer yet full of "Godly activity," howsoever well intended, is a formula sure to fail. Again his concreteness is accessible to anyone and in a disarming way gets right to the point without fanfare. How the life of the parish abets or fails to enliven one's interior life is also a worthwhile part of his reflections.

I would hope that people read Henry's book with his enthusiasm so that the good work that has begun in his heart and in the hearts of many by the action of the Holy Spirit "will be completed on the day of the Lord Jesus." (Ph 1:6)

Rev. John C. Haughey, S.J.
Catholic Business Guild
Charlotte, NC

The Word

Upon disembarking Jesus saw a vast crowd. He pitied them, for they were like a sheep without a shepherd; and he began to teach them at great length. It was now getting late and his disciples came to him with a suggestion: "This is a deserted place and it is already late. Why do you not dismiss them so that they can go to the crossroads and villages around here and buy themselves something to eat?" "You give them something to eat," Jesus replied. At that they said, "Are we to go and spend two hundred days' wages for bread to feed them?"

"How many loaves have you?" Jesus asked. "Go and see." When they learned the number they answered, "Five loaves and two fish." He told them to make the people sit down on the green grass in groups or parties. . . Then taking the loaves and fishes, Jesus raised his eyes to heaven, pronounced a blessing, broke the loaves, and gave them to the disciples to distribute. He divided the two fish among all of them and they ate until they had their fill. They gathered up enough leftovers to fill twelve baskets, besides what remained of the fish. Those who had eaten numbered five thousand men (Mk 6:34-44).

About This Book

This book is about a living miracle—you. You live and work in the world but you are different. You are a Christian, a person transformed by God's Spirit. You bring to the marketplace a different agenda formed in the light of God's love.

Miracle in the Marketplace is a call to reflect on the real role of lay Christians in the world, where they belong. They belong in the world because they are born into the world, and they are called by Jesus to love as he loves, to heal the sick, to comfort the afflicted, to free the imprisoned, to feed the hungry and to give hope to the despairing.

Maybe you feel inadequate for such a task. One goal of *Miracle in the Marketplace* is to help you discover your strengths and the gift you are from God to the world.

If you feel inadequate, imagine yourself as one of the disciples in the scripture passage on the preceding page. You are facing more than 5,000 hungry people. Jesus tells you: "You give them something to eat."

How can you feed all those people with little money and less food? How in the world could Jesus be so unreasonable and unrealistic?

"How much bread do you have?" Only five loaves of bread and two fish. Here is the power of this gospel scene: Jesus took what the disciples had, as little as it was, and he made it more than enough! After everyone had their fill, there was enough bread left to fill 12 baskets, plus the leftover fish.

The message is very clear. Jesus is telling us: Give me what you have, no matter how insignificant you think it is, and I will multiply your gift just as I multiplied the insufficient food and faith of my first disciples. Give me yourself, in faith, and you will become a miracle in the marketplace.

So often lay people hesitate to share their faith or tackle thorny social problems because they feel so limited, so inade-

8

quate. This book is meant to encourage everyone, but particularly lay people, to give what they have so Jesus can work miracles. Here indeed is a call to a renewed sense of lay mission in the world—a mission of presence and service—sent into the world by a parish with a broadened vision of Church.

Catholics experience Church in their parishes where they should find inspiration, education and motivation for the fundamental mission given by the Lord. If they do not find this support in their parishes, many will never experience the joy, thrill and fulfillment of their vocations in the world.

I will be suggesting here the formation of a new parish ministry, the Marketplace Mission Group through which parishes may give priority to the mission of lay people in the world.

How to Use This Book

People who cannot spend long hours reading, can read this book in "snatches" on buses, trains, airplanes, at lunch time or on the run between chores and trips to school or the supermarket.

The reflections at the end of each chapter will benefit all readers, but especially those who want to use *Miracle in the Marketplace* for a more leisurely and organized approach to spiritual growth.

These reflections can be used by individuals or groups. Each reflection contains an inspirational reading, quiet prayer and reflection, starter questions (for both personal and group meditation), a commitment to a specific action which readers will decide for themselves, and a closing prayer.

The group reflections may be used, for example, by couples, prayer partners, or possibly small groups in parishes as a follow up to the RENEW program. They can also benefit parish councils, adult education classes, service commissions and prayer groups. These reflections may be used as a follow up to Cursillo, Marriage Encounter, Kairos and Baptism in the Spirit through the Charismatic Renewal. They may be especially helpful to Franciscan, Dominican and Carmelite Third Order groups.

I suggest, however, that in group sharing, some time be allowed for private reflection before group discussion.

To benefit most from individual reflection, designate a regular prayer time and a special place in which to read, pray and reflect. Many Christians find it beneficial to use a holy picture or icon, a lighted candle and an open Bible or some other meaningful symbol as a way to designate visibly their prayer place as holy. Music, for many people, is an aid to prayer. This special time is made holy by consecrating it to God. Let nothing but a real emergency disturb this time set aside for you and God.

10

The command of Jesus is urgent: "YOU give them something to eat." Every Christian, every day, meets people suffering from hunger—hunger for food, love, happiness, fulfillment and meaning in life. Every Christian is a living word of hope, peace, forgiveness and love from God, and when we give of ourselves, we grow stronger in these virtues and gifts.

To prove your love for Jesus, you must do what Jesus tells you to do (See Jn 14:21).

You are called by Jesus to be a miracle of love and hope in a world desperate for both.

Deacon Henry Libersat
Lent 1990

PART I

The Catholic Laity —
A Personal Agenda

*Whatever you do, work at it with your
whole being. Do it for the Lord rather than for
men, since you know full well you will receive
an inheritance from him as your reward. Be
slaves of Christ the Lord.   (Col 3:23-24)*

Chapter One

A Personal,
Not Private, Agenda

Many lay people don't feel they can be active in "Church work" because they are so involved with the concerns of everyday life.

Lay people will say, "If only I had more time. I'd really love to work for the Church, but I simply can't."

Please! Once and for all, let's put aside false notions about lay people and their "work" in and for the Church.

If you are a baptized Christian, if you have faith in Jesus Christ and try to love and serve him and the people around you, *whatever you do* is "Church work" If you drive nails or a big truck, if you fill prescriptions or diagnose diseases, if you program computers or act on a stage, if you report news or work in a government office, if you are a chef in a restaurant or a homemaker cooking family meals—you are doing "Church work" because you *are* the Church.

Pope Paul VI, in his moving 1975 document *On the Evangelization of Peoples* makes it very clear: lay people evangelize by their very presence in the world. Because God lives in you, everything you do has the potential of making his presence known to others.

I knew a man who for most of his life was a lay person. Just four or five years before his death, he became a permanent deacon. His greatest contribution to the Church was his life in the world as a manager of a retail store. He was a very kind, gentle and loving person. He "preached" Jesus without banging on a Bible or waxing eloquent on theology. He simply loved and people were transformed by his life.

Nearly three decades have passed since Vatican Council II and still the Church (and that means all of us, priests and laity alike) has not successfully motivated and activated the Catholic laity for their mission of healing and loving in the modern world.

In the documents of Vatican Council II, the bishops of the world, with the Holy Father, captured the vision of a people of God changing the world through their involvement in the marketplace, in the home, in the local schools.

Catholic lay people must realize and believe with all their hearts that what they do from nine to five and on weekends with their families is as much a Catholic activity as is attendance at Mass. Their "worldly concerns" are God's concerns, the Church's concerns.

A very dear friend has earned a living both in the world and in the Church. I asked him what concerned him most in his life as a lay Christian working and living in the world. He listed three things:

1. He said he needs to know that what he is doing every day is important to the mission of Christ. He is a man whose faith has cost him money. He sells insurance and retirement programs and he said he will not "tell people what they want to hear just to make a sale." Lying is wrong so he doesn't lie. He said that he feels he is as thoroughly Christian when he is selling as he does when he sings in the parish choir. He said he needs the support of his fellow Christians who also work in the world.

2. His greatest disappointment and a serious concern in his life are fellow parishioners who go to church on Sunday but forget their commitment to Jesus during the week. "Somehow," he said, "we have to help these people develop a closer relationship with Jesus and try to get them

to open themselves to the power of the Holy Spirit."

3. My friend, 55 years of age and father of several grown
    children, said he was also concerned about his children
    whose values differ significantly from his own. He was
    especially concerned about his children who no longer go
    to church.

I have worked full time in the Church for more than 30
years and I would probably have more difficulty than he in
surviving out there in "the world."

My friend is at home in the world—as are most lay people.
Even with all its problems, it is a wonderful place in which to
live, a home which his children and mine must make their
own, improving it as they can, building on what their parents
and grandparents left them.

Concerns of God's People

In the thirty years I've been a working journalist in the
Catholic press, I've interviewed many people. Their hopes,
joys, sorrows, needs and desires were all part of the story of
the Church as reported in the pages of newspapers,
magazines and books.

Lay people are concerned about many things. They want
their lives to be meaningful and useful. They want to be
good, honest and dependable. They want to be good friends
to others and they want to have dependable and loyal
friends.

Lay people want adequate pay. They want to be treated
fairly. They want meaningful work, happy marriages, healthy
and peaceful families. They want security in their old age,
families who will still love them and not hide them away, out
of sight and out of mind.

People want to protect their children from criminals, sin,
drug and alcohol abuse. They want "the Church" to inspire
them to greater holiness, to remind them that life is worth

living and assure them they can make the world even better.

Lay people want to know and love God more intimately and fruitfully.

These are "Church concerns," every last one of them.

Catholic News Service in Washington, D.C., made a wonderful contribution in 1990 with its *Faith Alive* series published in many diocesan newspapers around the country. Part of the series dedicated to the role of lay people in the world, reported the experiences of lay people who discovered, in their work-a-day world, the opportunity to live and spread the gospel through their skills and ordinary relationships.

Each Christian's strengths and weaknesses affect the entire Church. The beautiful gift of preaching given a Bishop Sheen, Billy Graham or Sister Briege McKenna benefits the entire Church. The gift of teaching—from the pulpit and the teacher's desk in the local public or private school—benefits the mission of the Church.

At the same time, people's individual needs are the needs of the entire Church. Lonely elderly, confused youths, overworked single parents, burned-out pastors, those who suffer unresolved anger or grief—all are sufferings of the Church. All are in need of healing. Suffering unattended is failed Christianity. Suffering alleviated, or at least shared, leads to liberation and a confirmation of confessed faith.

Your own personal agenda—all your daily concerns, hopes and fears—is part and parcel of the Church's presence and mission in the world.

In the hilarious movie *Nine to Five* the point about personal agenda is well made. The movie is about three women who decide to do something about their male chauvinist boss. Through a series of mistakes, they end up having to hold the man prisoner while they run the company. They change policies to help meet the needs of employees. They begin a day care center for young children and repaint the offices and store rooms in bright, lively colors. They encourage employees to have potted plants and other cherished, personal items in their work space.

Most Catholics, and perhaps most other committed Christians, would not consider such innovative leadership in an office "Church work." But when Christians better the world, it is Church work. When the world is made better it is because there has been healing or enlightenment or conversion—or all three—and these are like little "miracles" to those freed through the work of Christians.

A Need for a New Emphasis

Generally speaking, lay people have yet to discover the spiritual power they have to change the world.

In baptism, each Christian begins to live God's own divine life. The Christian shares in the eternal and all-powerful priesthood of Jesus Christ, becomes, in a sense, a living gospel bringing Jesus into work, business, politics and economics.

In many parishes around the country, lay people have become very active in official parish ministries. They are lectors, special ministers of the Eucharist, ministers to the sick and so on. They have been accepted and encouraged to participate in these parish ministries, but I'm afraid we would find very few Catholic parishes in the United States in which lay people are told about their mission in the world and are affirmed and enabled in that mission.

Parishes are still engaged in the maintenance of their own structures—and those structures must be maintained. The parish is the place we all gather for renewal, for the sacraments, for Eucharist, for gathering and worshipping with the faith family.

The mission, however, is "out there in the world," that world so loved by God that he sent his only Son to die for it (Jn 3:16).

Personal but Not Private

The lay person's agenda is truly a "personal" one, but it is not a totally "private" one. The personal agenda is filled with things which involve both our secular and religious needs: the desire to grow in holiness and to become financially responsible and independent, the desire to improve one's working conditions and family situation, the desire to become better educated and skilled on the job, the desire to spend leisure time in a creative and fruitful way, the desire to be truly happy and to share our faith.

Several things happen when a parish realizes that the personal agenda and the concerns of all parishioners are truly part of the parish agenda.

1. The individual receives caring attention from the parish family including the official ministry of the parish. His or her strengths and gifts are affirmed and become fully integrated into the overall mission of the parish. The parish mission is rooted in Jesus' great commission, "Go and make disciples of all the nations" (Mt 28:19). In other words, bring the gospel into the secular community in which it lives.

    If personal agendas become part of the community agenda, individuals more easily get the help they need to change problems into opportunities and oppressive situations into experiences of liberations. For example, if parish homilists are attuned to the mission of lay people in the world, their Sunday messages take on a more universal perspective—beyond the boundaries of parochial projects and needs. Educational programs will help people relate their faith more directly to their work and community services.

2. The parish is made stronger by the realization that it has the *power* to change things—that God does make good on his promise to answer prayer and to help people who try to do what is right. It does little good to complain about "the

world" and condemn all the evil in it. A more creative and Christian approach is to develop ways in which to offset the evil with good. For example, instead of just complaining about pornography, why not organize public demonstrations against "adult entertainment" establishments or develop programs to help people kick the porn habit and addiction to sexual abuses? It is, after all, the Christian's responsibility to help heal those afflicted by emotional problems and/or sin.

3. People outside the parish will *see* faith and not just hear about it. One of the most serious criticisms that can be leveled against the Church is the charge that we do not practice what we preach. We urge civic leaders to be just, but we are often slow to take sides in sticky issues—such as fighting for just and fair treatment of illegal migrants. And it does us little good to preach justice when parishes or dioceses are unjust in their treatment of employees and minorities. As more lay people begin to take an active role in establishing justice in the marketplace, and are openly encouraged to do so by their bishops and priests, the rest of society will find the entire Church more credible.

4. Every parishioner, knowing that his or her personal agenda is part of the parish agenda, will gain both strength and perspective in sharing their faith and helping other people who are in need. Acceptance and recognition in a community helps a person overcome timidity, anxiety and uncertainty. This support enables her or him to be loving and affirming. I know a woman who had a strong personal faith, but was afraid to share it. She joined a parish in which she was loved and affirmed. She was given an opportunity to share her faith in a small group. Once she had experienced acceptance she began to blossom and now she is a powerful witness of faith in the marketplace.

5. The mission is shared by more people, not just the 10 to 15 per cent of the laity who are presently involved in Church

work. The Church becomes more effective and credible because there is clearer vision, greater unity and shared commitment to the mission of the Church.

One example comes to mind. It shows the kind of imagination that can transform parish-oriented ministry into world-oriented ministry.

The young adults in a suburban parish wanted to do something for their peers (not necessarily members of their parish) who were trapped in "the singles bar scene." They began a ministry called the *Lamp Post Cafe*, a once-a-month dinner dance which served only non-alcoholic beverages.

The young adults in this parish ministry spent a lot of time each month converting the parish hall into a respectable restaurant. They wore uniforms, had professionally printed menus, volunteered their time in set-up, cooking, serving and clean-up.

They never preached, but invariably the guests would inquire about their "job" and how much they were paid to work at the *Lamp Post Cafe*. When the guests were told that all workers were volunteers who spent at least ten hours working in the ministry each month in addition to their full-time jobs, they would be surprised and ask "Why do you do that?"

The young adult ministers would sit down at the table and explain their desire to live good and wholesome lives. They would tell the guests how faith in Jesus and belonging to his Church helped them achieve these goals. Because of this low-key ministry and its respect for the people it served, several people were brought back into the Church and many more were strengthened in their faith.

These young Catholic people saw a need—the desire others had for companionship without the sordid atmosphere of a singles bar—and met that need.

That is catholic, holy and evangelistic. Now take that same desire to help people through a parish ministry and apply it to the marketplace. I'm a regular customer in a pizza place in

Orlando. I go there two or three times a week. It's a most un-usual place because of the waiters and waitresses. Pearl, one of the waitresses, is a favorite among all the customers. She knows customers by name, knows where they want to sit, how rushed they usually are. She accommodates the cus-tomers. People are not just objects to be seated and fed pizza and diet colas. Each person is made to feel as though she or he is someone special—and of course each person is some-one special.

In the same restaurant is a young man named Obie. He is a musician but he can't find a steady job playing trombone. He works at serving pizza to support himself while he con-tinues to look for that dream job. He could be bitter and self concerned, but he seems to take great pleasure in serving the customers. He, too, knows many customers by name and works cheerfully to meet their needs.

Al, the day manager, helps set an atmosphere in which the waitresses and waiters can concentrate on the needs of people. He is warm, friendly and genuinely concerned about people. He helps bus tables and when someone makes a mis-take, he quietly steps in to make things right.

Going to this pizza place in the middle of a hectic workday is refreshing and healing because the workers there are con-cerned with more than merely "making a living." They want to make people happy. I think what they do for people is a real Christian service. Their faith has given them a context in which they can relate to everyone as friend, as equal, as spe-cial. Many different kinds of customers come into that little place of business—clerks, secretaries, stock brokers, plumbers, students, truck drivers, nurses—and for a brief time they can relax, let their guards down, enjoy just being people among people.

I think Al, Obie and Pearl are truly graced and doing God's work, the Church's work. Through their daily care for others they are working little miracles in the marketplace.

REFLECTION

At the beginning of each reflection, remember to spend a little quiet time. Don't forget to select a special time and place to pray and reflect. Use a candle, Bible or icon to help you focus on the Lord Jesus.

Now, God gives us many kinds of special abilities, but it is the same Holy Spirit who is the source of them all. There are different kinds of service to God, but it is the same Lord we are serving. There are many ways in which God works in our lives, but it is the same God who does the work in and through all of us who are his. The Holy Spirit displays God's power through each of us as a means of helping the entire Church. . .

Now here is what I am trying to say: All of you together are the one body of Christ and each one of you is a separate and necessary part of it. (1Cor 12:4-6,27)

Quiet Time

In the light of this reading, reflect for a few moments on what you have just read about the personal agenda as a concern for the entire Church.

Prayer

Lord, Jesus, I want to be open to all you want to give me and what you want me to give to you in and through your Church. Help me to understand how my personal life is really Church life. Amen.

Starter Questions

1. God does his work "in and through all of us *who are his*." Do I really believe that I am his, that he cares for me, wants me, even needs me to love him?

2. God's work in us "helps the entire Church." How can I
    develop a better understanding of how my personal agen-
    da is truly part and parcel of how God reaches out to the
    world through me and the rest of the Church?

3. Do our parish programs help people understand they are a
    necessary part of the Church and not just people who need
    the Church's ministry?

Commitment to Action

To help the people of our parish and our parish leadership
become more aware of how each personal agenda is part of
the Church agenda (I, we) will. . .

Prayer

"Ask and you will receive." These are your words, Lord
Jesus, and you live up to your promises. Please give us the
grace to love, enable, support and affirm everyone in our
parish. Amen.

Chapter Two

Overcoming
Obstacles to Belonging

St. Boniface Parish in Pembroke Pines, Florida, just eight miles north of Miami, has successfully involved hundreds of parishioners in the mission of the parish.

The pastor, Father Michael Eivers, and Deacon Perry Vitale spent months of study, reflection and research in trying to discover a model through which their parish might fulfill the divine mandate of Christ, "Make disciples of all nations."

The pair visited the internationally famous Evangelical pastor in Korea, Rev. Cho, who at that time had organized a congregation of some 200,000 into active cell groups who were evangelizing throughout Seoul.

They visited Baptist churches, Congregational churches and other Catholic parishes where small groups had already proved successful in various ways.

At home, small groups of parishioners were praying for efforts to develop their parish into a vibrant, evangelizing Christian community. Some members of the parish were already evangelizing door-to-door. Father Eivers himself pastored the Friday night charismatic prayer service attended by some 200 people; the parish's Sunday Masses were filled to overflowing with Catholics and Protestants; more than 250 families were sharing intercessory prayer before the Blessed Sacrament from 6 a.m. to midnight.

This is a rich and rewarding story and has been told in print elsewhere. The bottom line is this: Father Eivers, his associate pastors, the lay leaders and Deacon Vitale discovered that the real power of evangelization lay in two fundamental realities: small groups of Catholics, bound together in their eucharistic, sacramental faith, coming together to pray and grow in their faith, and the active participation of those Catholics in secular society as they live and apply their faith and love to their own environment.

The individual cell groups, now numbering approximately 50 in St. Boniface, meet in their homes every two weeks. They praise God, share their faith stories, intercede for the parish and reflect on the Sunday gospel by watching a video tape prepared by one of the parish priests and duplicated in the parish video studio.

The parishioners involved in the cell groups reach out to people in need in their neighborhoods, schools and work places. They are not "convert-hunting" as much as they are looking for opportunities to help people, but neighbors and co-workers who have been away from the Church for a long time are invited to come home. If a Protestant comes to their cell group and expresses a desire to return to his or her own church, they help that person contact the local pastor of the particular Protestant church.

Father Eivers' first priority is to bring people into a personal relationship with Jesus Christ and into the Catholic faith community if that is where they feel called. However, the cell groups go beyond a strictly parochial agenda. The cell groups help members become more sensitive to people's needs, encourage Catholic laity to love and help people in their neighborhoods and work place as well as to use their influence in the civic community.

Through the cell system, all people are incorporated into the mission of the parish; their Sunday liturgies are more meaningful because they have shared so much all week long; the entire parish has a strong sense of belonging; there is a lovely intimacy between priests and people which enhances and strengthens their respective roles.

The parish team has been invited to Europe and to various parts of the United States to give seminars on the cell system of parish growth and evangelization. Each year the parish hosts a conference on the cell system. The conference draws people from nearly all continents. The cell system has been adopted by parishes in several European countries and is beginning to make headway in rejuvenating a truly Catholic spirit there.

None of this happened in a vacuum. There was a pastor and his team who had a vision. There was a willingness to take chances, to look beyond where they were to where they could be. There was a deep spirit of prayer, centered in the Eucharist, and a true fidelity to the teachings of the Church and the authority of their own Archbishop Edward McCarthy of Miami who himself is deeply committed to Catholic evangelization. Also, Father Eivers was determined that the lay people of his parish would discover the power of their baptismal priesthood and learn how to use that power for the sake of the Gospel and the good of society.

The challenge for St. Boniface Parish—and every other parish in the world—is to continue to grow as an evangelizing parish and to help all parishioners realize they are truly Christian and evangelistic when they do well what they are called by God to do "in the world"—when they serve people and make the world better by being good and fair police officers and attorneys devoted to justice and the spirit of the law, nurses and doctors who recognize the dignity of the people they treat or teachers of science or math who approach their students with a sense of wonder over God and his limitless wonders.

There are surely other parishes throughout the nation who have discovered special ways in which to experience the breadth and depth of what it means to be a worshipping, evangelizing community of faith but we can't mention them all here. No doubt in every instance of success you will find at the heart of the parish a pastor and a staff who have been inspired by the vision of Vatican Council II and are free enough to encourage everyone to share in the mission and ministry of the Church.

Lay people have their own personal agendas. So do pastors and parish staff members. The secret to success lies in bringing all those agendas into community reflection in the light of the gospel, discover how each agenda fits into the mission of the Church, and develop a parish process through which the mission will be accomplished by shared faith, vision and ministry.

It is important for pastors and staff members to remember that the real place of the Church is in the world and that the mission of most of the faithful is in the world. That is why Father Elivers' parish cell system is so successful. He's affirming lay people where Jesus put them, in the world, ministering to and evangelizing what the Greeks called their *oikos*—their environment.

A Different Church

Today, Catholics' personal agendas run the gamut from preservation of natural resources, ecology, politics, economy, national security, foreign policy, welfare budgets, Little League, community youth activities and Third World problems to the more traditional Catholic concerns of religious education for the children, sufficient vocations to the priesthood, adequate funds for the parish and diocesan ministries.

We are no longer the immigrant Church which came to the United States in the midst of Catholic reaction to the Protestant Reformation. That reaction separated Catholics from their Protestant brothers and sisters, bred triumphalism and discrimination among both Protestants and Catholics.

Catholics coming into this country from Poland, Germany, France and other nations were often met with suspicion and even hatred. Catholics could not speak English; many were not educated. They came to depend on their priests—often the only educated men in the parish—to help them cope with harassment from the local Protestants, overcome discrimination in seeking jobs, understand legal papers and even communicate with relatives back in the old country.

In that setting, parish priests became real fathers to their people and the laity thrived on that paternal love and service. This paternalism and lay dependence became part of the institutional structure of the Church in America. It is hard to change something that has become ingrained in institutional structures. Following Vatican Council II, when lay people were asked to assume more responsibility in forming the directions for ministry, there was confusion and even resistance, so strong was the Catholic identity tied to that paternalistic, institutional experience of Church. Words and concepts such as community, collegiality and shared ministry were alien to Catholic understanding and experience.

One of the most significant changes springing from Vatican Council II is movement toward *community*. I realize people are tired of that word. It has been used and abused. It is still a good word, however, a word that speaks of a people who hold something in *common*, something so powerful and precious that it brings people into *unity*.

Unity in the Church is not the same thing as belonging to a fraternity. To belong to the Church is to belong to Jesus, to experience a personal transformation through the power of the Holy Spirit that changes all of one's life and touches all relationships.

To belong to the Church is to live the very life of God, to be made holy by him, to share his mission to bring all people into communion with him through Jesus Christ the Lord.

Community is a reality with many expressions. There are certain "buzz words" which relate to these expressions, such as collegiality (shared decision-making), subsidiarity (letting things be handled at the lowest possible level), dialogue (talking things over), and consensus (reaching decisions by prayerful reflection and agreement rather than by ballot).

The greatest expression of community, however, is not a smoothly running parish organization with people actively involved in parish tasks, but the love people show for each other in the parish and the love they individually and collectively, as a parish, show for the world in which they live.

Obstacles to Community

Failure to love is the primary obstacle to community. There are other obstacles as well, some of which are direct results of the failure to love: limited understanding of what faith means; isolationism and fundamentalism; stockpiling; clericalism, anti-clericalism, laicism and/or anti laicism.

Let's take a brief look at each of these obstacles to community.

Limited understanding of what faith means

Christian faith is belief in Jesus Christ as Son of God, Messiah and him crucified, dead and risen from the dead. This is the basic message the apostles preached, a message with such power and promise that thousands converted when they heard Peter's first sermon on Pentecost (Acts 2).

Sometimes, Catholics seem to place their faith in the external actions of religion—in certain forms of piety, for example. Sometimes they seem to place more faith in "the Church," its structures and institutional characteristics, than in the Lord Jesus himself. For some, doctrine becomes the all-consuming concern and the proof of whether a Catholic has faith or not. For some, the "rules" become a barrier to knowing a Jesus of compassion and mercy.

Piety is important, but it is far more than praying correctly. Piety is the gift of right relationship through which we can call all men and women our brothers and sisters in spite of real or imagined differences.

Doctrine is important, but it is not God. Doctrine tries to

capture in words, the truth which is God, the truth which is beyond words. Doctrines try to express what we have come to understand about God's revelation of himself and they, too, are important. Piety, doctrine, even the Church itself, apart from an active faith in Jesus Christ, have little meaning. If we do not accept Jesus and do not know him personally, we can never hope to discover the fullness of what it means to be made in God's image and to be fully human. Only Jesus can transform lives, change despair into hope, sorrow into joy and guilt into pardon. Accepting him as personal savior, believing that he would have died "just for me," makes all the difference in the world.

Another stumbling block comes with a misunderstanding of Tradition and tradition. To the Catholic, Tradition (big T) is as much a part of revelation as is the Bible. On the other hand, tradition (small T) is the way in which we have come to express and celebrate Tradition (big T). For example, it was a tradition in rural Louisiana for the priest to bless the crops after planting. Throughout our nation, for many years, it was traditional to have Forty Hours devotions and public processions on the feast of Christ the King.

When these traditions (small T) changed, some people were upset, but nothing central to the faith, no Tradition (big T), had changed: it was still God who made crops grow and we could pray to him without the blessing of fields; Jesus was still Christ the King even if we didn't march in a parade; Jesus was still really present in the Blessed Sacrament even if we didn't hold Forty Hours devotions.

Isolationism and fundamentalism

Some politicians try to please everybody by straddling the fence on major social and moral issues: "I'm personally against guns and abortion, but other people have the right to make up their own minds. After all, you can't legislate morality."

That's two things: a smoke screen and a lie. Being

personally against anything can mean only that you're against
it. How can you be against child abuse but say parents have
the right to abuse their children? Saying you're against an
evil but don't want to force your opinion on others is a smoke
screen to prevent yourself and others from realizing you really
haven't committed yourself to a principle.

And it is untrue to say, "You can't legislate morality." We
do it every day. Although we don't have a law to cover every
moral position, we cannot deny that laws do uphold certain
moral precepts. For example, it is immoral to abuse children,
to murder people, to steal, to drive under the influence of alcohol, to poison one's system with drugs, to mar the face of
nature by pollution and littering—and we have laws against
all these things.

What we are talking about is *isolationism*—separating
religious convictions, the power of faith and the commitment
to Christ from everyday life.

Isolationism would also block out the influence of different
and various cultures, strive to maintain the status quo in the
Church and in society even when the status quo is tradition
and not Tradition.

Then there is *fundamentalism*. Fundamentalism is not all
bad. We all have fundamentals to which we adhere. God is
Trinity. Jesus is Lord, Savior and Son of God. He died for
our sins, rose from the dead and is now at the right hand of
the Father. These are fundamental truths.

There is, however, a certain unhealthy fundamentalism
rooted in insecurity. This type of fundamentalism tries to har-
ness God's Word to mean specific things at specific times.
Fundamentalists speak of the "inerrancey of the Bible" and
insist that scripture is literal and cannot be individually interpreted, all the while interpreting scripture to support their
own limited understanding of God's Word.

There are Catholic fundamentalists, too. These find
security not in the person of Jesus Christ, but in the laws of
the Church, its doctrines and dogmas. Their faith is in expressions and formulas of faith, in words that try to capture for

the cultural and generational moment the meaning of truth. This fundamentalism borders on idolatry.

Both Catholic and Protestant fundamentalism, the unhealthy kind, are born of insecurity. Insecure people need firm, pat answers or they go to pieces. So they take doctrine or scripture out of context and knit for themselves a security blanket, pull it over their heads and blind themselves to further revelation of truth.

Fundamentalists cannot appreciate the various expressions of Church, how we all together, each with his or her own unique understanding, form the body of Christ which continues to reveal the Father.

For the fundamentalist, faith is static, certain. What they call "faith" is an attitude that at least borders on presumption: "Once saved always saved."

For the rest of us, faith is dynamic, alive, co-existent with doubt. Indeed, if there were no doubt, there would be no need for faith. In faith we focus on Christ who fully reveals the Father. We cannot grasp all Christ reveals in one sitting or in a million sittings. As great as God is so great are the truths revealed in Christ. If we non-fundamentalists have one basic "fundamental," it is Christ. We need Jesus Christ and we constantly embrace him. We know we fall, we sin, but we know he forgives. Because we sin, we know we cannot take salvation for granted—but because of Jesus Christ, we know we can be saved through his mercy. We are free to seek forgiveness. We are free to ignore his offer to forgive. The terrible truth is that we are free even to reject such great love and such a gift as salvation.

In faith, we live without knowing the future, realizing that God will answer our prayers, but in his own way which may not be our way.

Stockpiling

Until recent years, Catholics were not good at building community. We were hatched, matched and dispatched—

baptized, married and buried—and that was about all anybody expected from the Catholic Church. Surely nothing akin to evangelization was expected of the laity.

Evangelical and fundamental churches, on the other hand, caught the spirit of the gospel fellowship. Their converts were considered a vibrant part of their churches and were given responsibility to help the churches achieve their missionary goals.

Juan Carlos Ortiz, an Evangelical, really hit this point hard in a book called *Discipleship*. He said that many churches, and he accurately included the Catholic Church, were guilty of *stockpiling*.

He said there are two ways in which converts can be treated. They can be stockpiled like a bunch of bricks thrown helter-skelter into a heap, or they can be built into a church. When bricks are stockpiled, he said, an enemy can come along and steal bricks one at a time and the theft will go unnoticed for a long time. However, when bricks are built up into a church, each brick having a special place and function, a missing brick is noticed immediately.

The image is clear and a good one. Catholic parishes must learn that converts or returning Catholics have something to give the parish—and they want and need to serve.

Clericalism, anti-clericalism, laicism and anti-laicism

There is always a danger in disagreements that people will begin to divide into two camps: them and us. For the laity, "them" is the clergy and vice versa.

Clericalism is an attitude among the clergy that places them above everyone else. Simply because they are ordained; they have all the answers, know better than anyone else how things should be done, deserve the best of everything and the respect of the poor, unenlightened laity. Lay people, who put their priests on a pedestal, encourage this aloofness and make it difficult for their priests to develop healthy, intimate relationships in the community which would nurture them and enhance their ministries.

Anti-clericalism is an attitude, often in reaction to clericalism, that suspects and mistrusts men simply because they are bishops, priests or deacons. *They* naturally will never understand *our* viewpoint because they live in an ivory tower, have a hidden agenda, etc.

Laicism, akin to clericalism, gives lay people an exaggerated sense of importance and isolates them from the clergy. It often emerges as a reaction to clericalism. Sometimes, however, it arises from a certain pride and arrogance found among lay people who suddenly discover personal strengths and power, like teenagers who suddenly realize they are no longer children and aggressively assert their independence. Laity suffering with this malady, tend to ridicule the clergy and even treat their bishops and priests with contempt.

Anti-laicism is a reaction against laicism, but goes to the opposite extreme in which clergy may well mistrust all lay people as a group because of the abuse of a few or many lay people.

Even when these four undesirable attitudes do not exist in a parish, community is not easy to achieve. People may share an overall vision of service and evangelization, but they experience Church in different ways and disagree on how to achieve community and mission.

Models of Jesus and Church

Richard McBrien and Avery Dulles, two prominent priest-theologians in our own time, have developed "models" of how people experience Jesus and his Church. In other words, they hold up a mirror to all of us and say, "See, this is how *you* experience Jesus; this is how you experience Church."

In his excellent *Catholicism*, Father McBrien points to the many faces of Jesus.

Some see Jesus as *teacher*. For these people, orthodoxy is the utmost concern in faith and dissidents are the greatest threat.

Others see Jesus as *Ruler, King, Judge,* and these people see the Church as a royal court, perhaps enjoying much of the pomp, but their king, Jesus, rules with compassion.

Then there is Jesus, the *Holy Man of God.* Jesus and the Father are so holy, so far "up there" that we can't reach them. To be holy, you have to set the world aside (Janssenism), leave the world, because everything material is unholy.

Jesus is also *Liberator.* People who prefer to think of Jesus primarily as the champion and liberator of the poor may sometimes forget about the "kingdom yet to come." Their entire focus is on doing good here and now according to the social messages in the gospels. Little attention is paid to personal sin and the life to come.

I am reminded of one of my favorite stories about images of Jesus. I was ministering as a lay person in a Louisiana jail. One day I was speaking to a man who was in jail for getting into a drunken brawl. He was battered and bleeding. His bare feet were dirty, callused and bruised from the fight—and he was not interested in Jesus. Suddenly, it came to me that he wasn't interested in Jesus because he did not know that Jesus had truly become a man and suffered on earth as we suffer.

"Joe," I said to him, "Jesus had dirty toe nails."

The man's face registered surprise and then broke into a great big grin and he said, "He did?"

Joe was now ready to hear more about Jesus.

The following Sunday, I was having a rather tense discussion with an elderly parishioner who believed Vatican Council II had taken all the mystery and dignity out of Catholicism, to say nothing of the truth. We were talking about Jesus and I said to him, "Mr. B, did you know that Jesus had dirty toe nails?" It had worked for Joe, why not Mr. B?

Mr. B drew himself up to his full 5' 4", glared at me with utter disbelief and indignation and said, "Not MY Jesus," and turned on his heel and walked away.

One's image of Jesus is precious and personal and should never be tarnished by thoughtless arrogance. One's image of

Jesus can and should be broadened, however, through gentle and loving sharing of faith.

In his *Models of the Church*, Jesuit Father Dulles gives us five "models" of the Church.

There is the *Institutional Model*. People who experience the Church primarily as an institution believe the Church's main purpose is to bring us all into eternal life. The leaders of this model are the clergy. It is strong on structure and can easily breed clericalism. The "expert" in residence in this model is the pastor.

The *Community Model* would be more popular among people who captured the impact of Vatican Council II and felt personally inspired by the "new" concept of a people of God in love with him and one another. The purpose of the Church, in this model, is union with God. Its greatest strength is a sense of the presence and immediacy of the Holy Spirit and openness to his action in individual and community life. However, this model, by itself, would encourage spiritual narcissism, inordinate preoccupation with the community's own love, strengths, experiences and beauty. The expert in this model of Church is the ecumenist because he is trying to bring more and more people into the experience of one community in union with one God.

Some people experience the Church primarily as *Sacrament*. In this model, the purpose of the Church is to be a sign of God's presence in the world. People want their leaders to give witness to God's activity in their lives and in the Church. The expert here is the theologian. The danger in this model is that the people of God become too "spiritual," focusing all their attention and energy on being the spiritual presence of Jesus, looking down on "the world" and forgetting about the corporal works of mercy.

The Church is also experienced as *Herald*. In this model, the Church's main job is to proclaim the gospel. Its leaders are the preachers. It has a rich theology of the Word. Its experts are scripture scholars. Its chief danger is a certain neo-gnosticism. This neo-gnosticism expresses itself in people who seem to believe that knowledge of scripture and the ease and fervor with which one can quote it are signs of being saved and perhaps even the means by which one is saved. It is Jesus who saves, not our knowledge of him that saves us. It is conceivable that one could realize that Jesus is savior and still not submit oneself to him, know his Word and still not live it. Along with this false understanding of how salvation is experienced, there arises also a grave danger of exclusivity: "If you're not as excited about Scripture as we are, and understand it as we do, then you can't really be part of our community."

Finally, Father Dulles says, there is the *Servant* model. In this model, the Church's reason for being is to renew social structures, to liberate the oppressed, provide food for the hungry and equitably balance the supply and the use of natural and human resources. Its witness are the prophets; its leaders, social reformers. This model has immediate relevance to the poor of the world and cannot be ignored by the wealthy. However, left alone, the Servant model could lead people into secularism, a commitment to do good without faith in Jesus Christ and a share in his mission of salvation.

As though these differences in understanding Church were not enough to contend with, people also differ in how and why they respond to moral principles.

For example, you can take six "obedient" people and they can be obedient for different reasons. One fears punishment; another is obedient because of a promised reward; another person "feels good" when he does what is right; one enjoys the praise she received for being good; another is good because he perceived it as a duty; and still another will be obedient because she is convinced it is the right thing to do.

This last person has a mature sense of morality. She has made morality her own. She is convinced that what is right is right and she does it because it is right—not out of fear or selfishness or an external sense of duty, but because in conscience she cannot do otherwise.

I recommend that parish prayer groups, parish councils

and parish ministers participate in a retreat that covers models of church and faith, personality styles, group dynamics and levels of moral maturity. The understanding acquired from these shared experiences helps tremendously in bringing people together to achieve common goals and the common good.

I have participated in such retreats for prayer groups and for our staff at *The Florida Catholic*, a newspaper serving five of Florida's seven dioceses. It works.

Time now for a little reflection.

REFLECTION

Spend a few quiet moments gathering your thoughts.

That they may all be one; even as you, Father, are in me, and I in you, that they also may be in us, so that the world may believe that you have sent me (Jn 17:21).

There are different gifts but the same Spirit; there are different ministries but the same Lord; there are different works but the same God who accomplishes all of them in everyone. To each person the manifestation of the Spirit is given for the common good (1Cor 12:4-7).

I am the vine, you are the branches. He who lives in me and I in him will produce abundantly, for apart from me you can do nothing (Jn 15:5).

———————————

Quiet Time

How do these scripture readings relate to your experience of Church?

Prayer

Lord, Jesus, help me to become a loving person, one who helps others express their own faith stories, one who helps meet the needs of others to grow in love for one another and for God. Also, Lord, please help me to help others discover and use their gifts for your glory and the good of the world. Amen.

Starter Questions

1. What model of Church affords me most comfort; which makes me most uneasy?

2. In our parish, how do most people experience Church? Are all models expressed in our ministries, liturgies and relationships?

3. What concrete steps can (I, we) take in our parish to achieve greater unity through diversity?

Commitment to Action

To enrich (my, our) experience of Church and strive for greater unity among parishioners, (I, we) will . . .

Prayer

Change is not always easy, Lord, especially when we have to change ourselves. Help us all to seek interior change, personal repentance and renewal through the love of the Holy Spirit before we attempt to change others. Help us, too, to change undesirable social policies or structures which oppress us and our brothers and sisters. Amen.

PART II

Called and Chosen
A People Set Apart

You, however, are "a chosen race, a royal
priesthood, a holy nation, a people he claims
for his own to proclaim the glorious works" of
the One who called you from darkness into
his marvelous light. Once you were "no
people," but now you are God's people; once
"there was no mercy" for you, but now you
have found mercy.   (1Pt 2:9-10)

Chapter Three

Miracle in
the Marketplace

There is such power and beauty in life, in people going about their business, each pursuing a personal agenda, but all breathing the same air, driving the same highways, shopping the same stores, all being conceived, born and all someday dying, a massive movement of humanity from one day to the next. There is something paradoxical about us, about creatures equally adept at making love and war, healing and wounding, helping and hurting, laughing and crying.

Creation is a miracle and we are the miracle of all miracles—flesh, blood and bone, and spirit, too; instincts and subliminal drives, but the power to think, to choose, to love, a little like God. A paradox, to be sure, but a miracle none the less.

I'm enthralled by the miracle of humanity. I've "studied" us, in the markets of the Dominican Republic, Peru and Brazil, in the shops of Ostia and Rome, in the tight, ancient, stone streets of Jerusalem, in the shopping centers, malls and airports of Florida, Ohio, Illinois, New York, Connecticut, Texas, Louisiana, Arizona, California. I've studied us—all of us, moving from moment to moment, making noise and longing for silence, transforming everything in life and in the marketplace into a piece of the miracle of us.

Each of us, creature but also part creator, makes life

happen and we each give special meaning to the things of life: sales, bargains, charge cards, Christmas dinner, family reunions, job interviews, precious stones, movies and ball games, ski slopes and mountain trails, frozen lakes and blinding blizzards, ranches and farms, dirty clothes and garbage, gourmet foods and hot dogs, lemonade and beer and cold, fresh water. Everything is transformed in meaning because of us, because we first have been transformed by baptism, because we are now a people who is priest, prophet, royalty, holy. The miracle of baptism making possible the miracle of marketplace.

How does Jesus regard us, his people, sinners all?

What does he expect of us and how do we do his will in daily life, in the marketplace?

What mysterious power makes us different and able to change things and the meaning of things?

These questions are the heart of who we are as Christians, as people chosen individually and as a Church, to *be the presence of Jesus in the world*, maybe more, perhaps *to be Jesus in the world*.

Through the Eyes of Jesus

Sometimes Christians can forget they are so loved by the Lord that he would come to die for just one person who needed redemption.

It is easy to become overwhelmed with a sense of guilt and unworthiness. It is equally easy to forget that Christians are expected to strive for perfection, to pray and work to resist temptation and overcome habitual sin. I've personally experienced both extremes.

I want to share with you two scripture passages. Praying and reflecting on these passages can help the Christian see himself or herself through the eyes of Jesus.

The first is Psalm 139. This beautiful prayer of grateful praise and awe brings home with great gentleness the love

God has for each person. Pray with the psalmist. God has "probed" me and "knows" me. He was with me while I was "fashioned in darkness" and "knit" in my mother's womb. "He knows when I sit and stand."

But God does not love me alone. I am one of millions. What he tells me in this psalm he tells us all. He knows each of us and all of us.

He knows our thoughts even before we can form the words to express them. No matter how hard we try to find a place where he is not, he is there waiting for us when we get there—in the outer reaches of the heavens, at the most distant seashore. We cannot hide from him in darkness because he comes and he is light. We come to know him and realize how much he cares for us and we have to admit, somewhat breathlessly, that we are "fearfully, wonderfully made."

The second passage is Jn 15:15-17:

> *I no longer speak of you as slaves, for a slave does not know what his master is about. Instead, I call you friends, since I have made known to you all that I heard from my Father.*
>
> *It was not you who chose me, it was I who chose you to go forth and bear fruit. Your fruit must endure, so that all you ask in my name he will give you.*
>
> *The command I give you is this, that you love one another.*

It takes great faith and humility to be able to call Jesus a brother and friend as well as a God and judge. No person, without this beautiful revelation of the love of Jesus, could dare approach Jesus, the Son of God, as "friend."

Perhaps more than any other verse in scripture, this one, "I call you friends," challenged me and drove me to my knees while filling my heart with joy. Jesus could have loved me and even died for me without letting me know him as friend. He could have done all this only as my king and master, for indeed he is. But here, in John, he goes to great lengths to assure me, all of us, that we are each and together his friends.

He knows we will sometimes obey him and give him pleasure and at other times disobey and disappoint him. But he assures us, as he assured Peter on the beach after the resurrection (Jn 21:15 *ff*) that the sin of denial is not a terminal disease, that in spite of that sin, like Peter, we are still loved. Perhaps more importantly, the Lord let Peter prove to himself that he, Peter, could still love the Lord after sinning and that the Lord welcomed that love and rewarded it with a share in his mission.

So Jesus sees us as his friends, his co-workers, brothers and sisters in the same Father (God) and Mother (Mary).

What Jesus Expects of Us

The National Center for the Laity in Chicago is making a significant contribution to the Church's effort to define, in terms of Vatican Council II theology, the precise role of the laity in the Church in the modern world.

In 1986, the Chicago-based group published a working paper for a national consultation on the role of the laity. *The Power and Responsibility of Lay People in the World* made a prophetic observation: The special role of the laity "is to influence secular society from inside its social, cultural, political and economic systems. The laity are the key social action agents of the Church in the world. We are the 'religious insiders' who encounter God's grace and creative power in our businesses and our politics; in offices and factories; in homes and schools—in all events of our daily lives. Our commitment is to participate in secular life and reflect the grace that is contained in those experiences. In order to do this, however, we need to develop new ways of reinforcing our mission and sharing our experiences because our Church does not provide them now" (*Origins*, Sept.11, 1986, Vol.16, No.13).

Pope John Paul II, in his encyclicals on work, the laity and the role of the laity as evangelists has further developed the Vatican II theme that the primary role of the laity is in the world, acting as what Jesus called a "leaven," making the world whole through the love of Jesus.

The Holy Spirit is speaking clearly today through the Holy Father, the bishops and organizations like the National Center for the Laity.

It is clear that Jesus expects us to take the gospel seriously, to become bearers of the Good News which is God's love incarnate, to see our daily lives as sacred, holy and evangelistic, to overcome the temptation to separate "being Catholic" from being workers, lovers, builders and healers.

I think it is clear that Jesus expects Catholic laity to assume responsibility for his mission in the world. By and large, the laity are not doing that. In its 1986 document, the National Center on the Laity said, "The hope that Vatican II would herald a new age of the laity has not yet been fulfilled despite the great growth of lay ministries. These are valuable contributions, but there is a danger that this trend will become a new clericalism obscuring recognition of the fact that the vocation of the vast majority of Catholics is in and to the secular world."

This warning is given flesh by Report No. 11 of the 1987 *Notre Dame Study of Catholic Parish Life.* David C. Leege reveals some worrisome statistics in "Catholics and the Civic Order: Parish Participation, Politics and Civic Participation" (Institute for Pastoral and Social Ministry and the Center for the Study of Contemporary Society, University of Notre Dame).

Leege reports that of church-going Catholics who responded to a survey, almost 51 percent do not participate in any parish activities besides Mass and devotions and nearly 57 percent do not participate in any civic activities. Only about 27 percent of all Catholics responding to the survey were at least minimally involved in both parish and civic activities.

The Notre Dame study also discovered that women are

more active in parish activities than are men and that men are more active in civic concerns than are women. While among Catholics there is a slightly larger percentage of two-earner families than among Protestants, it is believed the women's jobs, "lack the status and the earning power of their husbands' jobs, and that their jobs are less likely to involve them in the web of community organizations."

Pope John Paul II in his encyclical, *On Human Work*, calls Catholics to a new vision of "work." Work is not simply what you do for a paycheck. Work is every human endeavor, including play. I have come to understand that "work" is anything in which I use my time, energy, body and mind—including prayer. The pope says that all human work has great dignity and must be seen as part and parcel of building up the kingdom of God.

The kingdom of God is something more than what most Catholics envision. The kingdom of God is more than the Church. Jesus mentions "Church" only twice in the New Testament—but he speaks frequently of the kingdom of God. Jesus founded the Church, no doubt about that, but it was a Church committed to building up the kingdom of God, a Church that embraced all of humanity and all of creation as part of the kingdom of God.

Pope John Paul does not see work as punishment for original sin but as an essential part of salvation and our participation in creation, in the building up of the kingdom. That's why it is Christian and "Church work" to drive buses and nails, to cook, to sew, to paint, to collect garbage, to practice law, to keep the peace, to vote, to run for office, to serve in public positions and so on. That's why Pope John Paul refers to the basic Christian way, the basic role of the laity as a "spirituality of work." That's why, in his encyclical, *Christifideles Laici*, the pope cautions the laity about two temptations—the temptation to see parish involvement as the ultimate expression of lay ministry and the temptation to separate Gospel values from daily living.

With this new focus on the role of the laity, we can

develop a deeper, more pertinent and more precise understanding and application of Jesus' great commission, "Go,
therefore, and make disciples of all nations" (Mt 28:19).

We are the miracle in the marketplace—human beings
transformed by the Holy Spirit into the real presence of Jesus
who, through us, continues to preach, to teach, to heal and
to proclaim the kingdom of God in our generation.

REFLECTION

For this reflection, I think it is better to begin with a little
quiet time.

Quiet Time

What does it mean to me to be a friend of Jesus, to have
Jesus as my friend? Do I believe he walks and works with me
at home and work? Do I believe I am a miracle in the
marketplace, that all of us together can make the world better
here and now—and invite more people into eternal life?

Prayer

Father, I am "fearfully and wonderfully made!" For this I
am truly grateful. Help me to be like Jesus, to love as he
loves, to be his eyes, ears, heart and hands reaching out to
my brothers and sisters. Amen.

Reading

*Humanity is able to hope. Indeed it must hope: The living
and personal Gospel, Jesus Christ himself, is the "good
news" and the bearer of joy that the Church announces each
day, and to whom the Church bears testimony before all
people.*

*The lay faithful have an essential and irreplaceable role in
this announcement and in this testimony: Through them the*

Church of Christ is made present in the various sectors of the world as a sign and source of hope and of love (Christifideles Laici, Origins, *Feb. 9, 1989, Vol. 18; No. 35).*

Starter Questions

1. Jesus, through his Church, tells us that we are each important to his mission in the world, that as his friends, we must love as he loves and treat people as he treated them. In the past week, how have (I, we) made the kingdom more visible through love and service to others? How have (I, we) failed?

2. What can we as Catholic lay people do together to heighten our awareness of our role in the world?

Commitment to Action

To help each parish member become more aware of the call of Jesus to be lovers of his world, (I, we) will . . .

Prayer

"I call you friends." Jesus, what wonderful news! Help us, Lord, to be good and true friends who love you enough to share your mission and sacrifice all, as you did, for the Father's kingdom. Amen.

PART III

The Challenge
You Give Them to Eat

*A new state of affairs today both in the
Church and in social, economic, political and
cultural life, calls with a particular urgency for
the action of the lay faithful. If lack of commit-
ments is always unacceptable, the present
time renders it even more so. It is not permis-
sible for anyone to remain idle.* (Christifideles
Laici, Op. cit, No.3)

Chapter Four

Marketplace
Mission Groups

In the winter of 1989-90, Europe, South Africa and the Soviet Union itself were the scene of dramatic change, of the defeat of oppression and the beginnings of democratic reform.

For people in the United States, the victories overseas were occasions that reminded us of our own fight for freedom in the Revolutionary War and in other wars throughout our history.

The triumph of Solidarity in Poland and of the African National Congress in South Africa, the tumbling of the Berlin Wall, the crumbling of Communist obstinacy in the Kremlin itself—all were tremendously inspirational for Americans and people throughout the world.

Christians may have been reminded, in those historical events, of the precious thirst for freedom which drives humankind to heroic behavior. We are, after all, created free, in the image of our God who knows no restrictions except that which he took upon himself—never to violate a person's free will and to become, in Jesus of Nazareth, like us in all things but sin.

The 1990s are going to present major challenges to Christians throughout the world. There will be the ever-present specter of famine, of civil war in poor and tottering nations, of the rape of virgin rain forests causing climatic imbalance worldwide, the ongoing challenge to free everyone from racial, sexual or religious prejudice, and the need to cement international and global ties in a shrinking and explosive world.

U.S. Christians, in the 1990s, will be further challenged to serve a growing number of persons living on inadequate incomes, people who find themselves jobless and homeless, single parents overwhelmed with the obligation to work and be both father and mother in a society beset with amoral influences and superficial religion. We will be dealing with a growing number of aged whose loneliness destroys their desire to live as well as their ability to find useful ways in which to serve the communities in which they live.

U.S. Christians in the 1990s must find a way to evangelize a nation which is Christian only in the romanticism of politicians and superficial preachers, to convince a nation addicted to noise and the quick fix that God loves and speaks in solitude and that there is value in suffering, that all human life is sacred, and that we all have a responsibility to protect our environment.

In a word, Christians in the 1990s will have to broaden their understanding of stewardship to include responsibility for all creation and the care and spread of the gospel message itself.

In the next decade, we Christians will have to embrace the world with greater love, develop more self confidence as graced men and women, and learn to let our faith permeate daily life at home, on the job and in the neighborhood.

This sounds like a tall order—and it is. No one person, no one group can do it alone. We all need each other to pull it off.

Three Levels of Response

We have to approach the problem on three levels—the personal, the local and the universal.

First, the personal level. Through baptism each Christian has the responsibility and grace to do what God wants that individual to do. Each Christian should be eager to have his personal agenda become a "mission agenda" which complements the missionary endeavors of other lay people, of the parish and diocese, and of the universal Church.

How can a person change his or her personal agenda into a "mission agenda"? Through personal and community prayer, reconciliation, Eucharist, spiritual direction and shared faith, and by consciously placing our personal agendas in the context of relationship with God and Church, we gradually begin to adopt a mission stance in all areas of our lives.

Just about everyone prays. Sometimes we don't feel we pray enough or regularly enough. Prayer must be a priority—and we must approach prayer as a time we are with Jesus and the Father and the Spirit rather than simply a time in which we speak with them. Christians who want to grow in their relationship with the Lord set aside a special time each day. Prayer must include praise, contrition, thanksgiving and petition. From what I hear, throughout the country more and more lay people are entering into contemplative prayer, the kind of prayer in which the person sits in silence before God and enters into a deep communion in which mind, heart and spirit are bathed by his gentle presence—all without words.

While personal prayer is essential to the Christian life, so is community prayer and community worship. When we gather together in prayer groups or at Mass on Sundays or weekdays, the Holy Spirit strengthens our faith in each other through communion with the Lord. It is in community prayer and worship that we first begin to tangibly experience the wonder of the communion of the saints. For saints we are, all of us, sometimes falling on our faces, sometimes weakening the communion by apathy, but always part of the Body of Christ through the Holy Spirit.

At Mass, through the power of the Holy Spirit, we are present on Calvary. We stand at the foot of the Cross and gaze upon the Lamb of God, upon the sacrifice which sets us free. It is not a new sacrifice, not a mere remembrance of that one sacrifice. The Mass transcends time and space, places us with Jesus, before the Father, at the site of our redemption. At Mass we experience personally and together, over and over again, what it means to be saved by the one sacrifice of Jesus Christ, what it means to be set free of sin and death and to gain eternal life.

Through the sacrament of reconciliation, the Christian experiences through ritual and faith the forgiving love of the Father and the joy of the Church in seeing one of her children reconciled with all the children of the Church. It saddens me that so many Catholics hesitate to take advantage of this great sacrament. After Vatican Council II, I had many difficulties with my faith and if I am still a Catholic, it is because I never stopped going to confession and Mass.

More lay people should have spiritual directors. A spiritual director can be a priest, deacon, religious or lay person of deep faith and training in spiritual direction. A spiritual director is a person who knows the spiritual life and can share their faith and help people discern God's will in their lives. The spiritual director does more listening and praying than advising.

A spiritual director is a sounding board, a confidant with whom our deepest desires and disappointments can be shared in faith, with a view to growth and healing. I've taken advantage of spiritual direction for more than 35 years and it has been a source of strength and growth for me.

Making a personal agenda become a mission agenda is easier if a person is sharing with others his or her struggles to serve God in the marketplace. Many Catholics have found it helpful to share faith through such movements as Cursillo and Marriage Encounter. Also, RENEW provides a structure in parishes in which a spiritual renewal process is employed. Some Catholics who work in the same office building, factory or neighborhood gather on a regular basis for breakfast or lunch to share prayer, experiences and hear a speaker.

Small group sharing strengthens individual faith and a

sense of community and shared mission.

Second, the local level. Parish priests and their staffs are responsible for enabling parishioners (the Church in the world) to fulfill their mission. The overall direction of the parish must be one of service and outreach into the general community while continuing the programs and worship needed to strengthen the faith community.

The parish staff has a prophetic, teaching, healing, unifying and affirming ministry to the people of God. The priest and staff serve prophetically by holding up to Gospel light the conditions of the faith community and secular community in which the parish lives and worships.

The parish staff may also fulfill its prophetic role by encouraging and facilitating dialogue between leaders and citizens of the secular community and the faith community. One idea may be to host a luncheon for area leaders to discuss important issues. Or, the parish staff could initiate a write-in campaign to encourage local community leaders to respond morally and justly to community needs. By putting a little creative thinking into such a project, any parish staff could come up with a successful way to encourage dialogue for the sake of the common good.

The parish staff teaches through its regular education programs and also by "stroking" its parishioners. Pastors traditionally congratulate and compliment only those lay people who are involved in official parish ministries or in special services to the parish—CCD and school teachers, the school principal, the president of the parish council, the choir director, the ministers to the sick, the parish festival committee.

This sends a false message to lay people: To be a *good* Catholic lay person, you have to be involved in parish ministry.

If pastors could expand their vision a little more and keep informed about the things lay people are doing *in the world* and compliment them from the pulpit, lay people would begin to embrace their mission in the world with more

eagerness and hope. If parish staffs begin to design programs
to help lay people fulfill their mission in the world, the laity
will be less timid and more successful in transforming the
world.

The parish priests and staff foster parish unity first of all
through forming a spirit of community among themselves,
while focusing all programs and ministries on the overall
parish community. It is extremely important to the life of the
parish and its mission in the world to be sure there is *one*
parish community. In many Florida parishes, there is a growing culture explosion as large numbers of Hispanics, Haitians,
Asians and Orientals immigrate into the state. In developing
ministries for these special groups—as well as for the hearing
impaired, the youth and the elderly—alert pastors and lay
ministers have to be careful to protect parish unity.

The entire parish family is enriched spiritually and
strengthened for its mission in the world when all groups
within the parish are nurtured according to their needs and,
at the same time, when all their gifts and differences are fully
integrated into the parish life and liturgy.

The parish staff heals by fostering a spirit of reconciliation
in the parish, helping the entire faith community to liturgically
celebrate repentance for personal and community sin. The
staff also serves as healer through communal anointing of the
sick and by urging parishioners to pray with one another for
physical or spiritual healing. Sometimes parishioners feel
awkward when asked to pray *with* others rather than simply
for them. The parish staff can help people overcome this
hesitancy through workshops and parish healing services.

Third, the universal level. The Holy Spirit moves
throughout the entire Church, speaking through laity as well
as clergy, through peasants as well as cardinals. The Church's
official teachers—the pope and the bishops—have the
responsibility of guiding the Church as it discerns what the
Spirit is saying. If a spirit of openness and collaboration per-
meates the universal Church along with obedience to God

and the teachers of the Church, the Church will be able to respond well to the challenges of the times and the needs of the world.

In our generation, there has been a growing tension between the magisterium and certain theologians. There has also been a lot of dissent against certain moral and social teachings of the magisterium among large numbers of laity.

It seems to me that a lot of dissension among the laity arises from misinformation about what the Church is teaching and why. We need to adopt a collaborative attitude that will help overcome the internal difficulties in the Church. We need a more open attitude toward persons in authority. At the same time, decision-makers need to listen with compassion and respect to those who struggle to understand and obey.

Perhaps many Catholics hesitate to tackle the world's problems because the problems seem so big. Even local community problems tend to overwhelm individuals. Catholic lay people often don't feel they have the authority to do anything about the problems of the world so they don't act without being officially told to do something specific. I think, too, that a mistaken understanding of separation of Church and state has discouraged lay people from flexing their political muscle in local and national concerns. Catholics have been intimidated by a vocal minority of fundamentalists who scream when the Church addresses political issues of moral consequence. Some of these same fundamentalists, however, have no qualms about endorsing a candidate who pleases them and using their own pulpits to play politics.

It doesn't take a papal directive to enable a Catholic to try to bring peace into an office torn by resentment, hate and misunderstanding. It doesn't take a parish program to authorize a Catholic to hold a bereaved co-worker while she or he cries with a broken heart. It doesn't take a pastor's permission to work on community projects designed to stamp out pornography, to feed the poor and to house the homeless.

For example, in Long Island, New York, what was initially

a small group outreach to the hungry has grown into the Interfaith Nutrition Network (INN), a not-for-profit organization that oversees 16 soup kitchens where 1,200 volunteers minister to almost 2,000 people daily. Moreover, The INN now provides temporary housing for the homeless in eight shelters. Besides a roof over their heads and food for their stomachs, The INN refers their "guests" to social workers, job counselors and medical resources. It is now attacking the systemic causes of poverty and is actively involved in acquiring permanent, affordable housing for the working poor through a combination of government, civic and church sponsorship.

The point is this: lay people on mission soon develop a network of relationships with other socially-conscious people and with government agencies and civic organizations. It should be obvious that Catholics working together can do more good for the world than can individuals working separately. When Catholics work together, I think it is important, if not essential, for them to be tied into the parish community in some way.

I am suggesting a parish-based movement in the marketplace, so that the laity and clergy will develop a stronger and clearer sense of the Church's mission in the world. Both clergy and laity would more easily see themselves as the Church "in the world" and their work as part of God's ongoing work of creation, redemption and healing.

With the mission rooted in the parish, it will be more easily perceived as rooted in Eucharist and as a work of the Body. Also, people will begin to relate "spiritual concerns" to "daily concerns." There need not and should not be a "war of the worlds" (spiritual and secular) going on in people's hearts. Once the two worlds are reconciled and united in a deeper understanding of "kingdom," people will be better able to respond automatically and wholeheartedly to the call to heal and love in the world, to evangelize and to work for justice in all social structures.

Marketplace Mission Groups

I suggest that parishes throughout the nation form what I would call Marketplace Mission Groups. These groups would provide support, direction and enrichment for lay people on mission in the marketplace. The groups would assist lay people in developing a truly lay spirituality—a spirituality of work, recreation, family and community. They would help to prepare and support lay people in identifying and meeting their needs—their personal agendas—and organizing them to serve the community—near and far.

Marketplace Mission Groups, as I see them, would help lay people exercise their particular mission of witness, love and service in their homes, on their jobs and in the community at large. This broadening of parish vision would inculcate a strong sense of Christian community as well as provide channels for more meaningful communication between the Church and the secular community.

I envision bi-weekly meetings where lay people would gather to reflect on the needs of the community, the individual's personal mission agendas and their experiences in trying to live as Christians in the world. They would encourage one another in their mission through their private and community prayer. Whenever possible, each Marketplace Mission Group would include a cross section of Catholic parishioners with diverse life styles—doctors, service people, domestics, managers, clerks, teachers, single parents, retirees as well as married couples. Clergy would be on an equal status with the rest, learning from the laity what it means to be Church in the world. Such a diverse group would better represent a multitude of personal agendas and at the same time provide a wealth of ideas, perspectives and skills. Such diversity underscores the need for a unifying medium—a gracious God—who provides such rich and varied gifts among his faithful and who continues to guide them in transforming the world.

The meetings would have to be carefully facilitated so that

they do not become gripe sessions, group counseling sessions or only "parish" related. The emphasis and focus has to be outward, striving to develop a deep personal spirituality with a global outlook. Marketplace Mission Groups can foster and fulfill our desperate attempts to touch and feel God's dynamic presence at work in the world.

A Success Story

As a universal Church, we are called to consider how our actions impact on the rest of humanity.

Father John Haughey, S.J., in St. Peter's Parish, Charlotte, N.C., has a success story. This Jesuit priest helped form the Catholic Business Guild in 1986. The guild meets regularly to discuss various community and justice issues. For example, they researched the problem of increased sales of American tobacco to Third World countries where people are not aware of the health hazard and tobacco companies are not required to include warnings on cigarette packs. They discussed the types of advertising used to encourage smoking and the complete lack of concern for the welfare of the people in Third World countries.

They addressed the following questions:

1. At what point do the health effects of cigarette smoking become an overriding ethical issue in a firm's decision-making?

2. How can individual responsibility be exercised in a situation where organizational action and responsibility is involved?

3. Should governments regulate personal habits that happen to have harmful effects?

It is quite clear that these are practical questions designed to help Catholic business persons apply their faith, education, experience and skills to a very important marketplace question that involves consumers, government, industry and advertising.

The Catholic Business Guild also tackled a local power plant which produced nuclear weapons. The Guild entered into dialogue with the local power company, hearing its side of the story and sharing their views as concerned citizens.

This is one example of how lay people can make an impact on society.

In the Diocese of St. Augustine, Florida, Bishop John J. Snyder is developing a training program and a liturgical ritual for commissioning lay people for their mission in the marketplace.

Catholics must be reminded over and over again that through their secular jobs, their recreation and their family life, they are indeed renewing the world. A handy little book many people could benefit from reading is *Confident & Competent, A Challenge for the Lay Church*, by William Droel and Gregory Augustine Pierce (ACTA Publications, Chicago).

In that book, we find the following: "At the heart of a work-centered spirituality is the relationship of the perfection of things and institutions on the one hand and the perfection of human beings on the other. The first aim of work is to bring creation toward perfection. . . . The second aim of work, however, is the completion, harmonization and realization of the worker. The perfection of creation must include the perfection of the person doing the work. To finish a job, to do work well, to bring things into perfection, takes more than technical skill. It takes a sense of ownership of the work being performed, a pride in its execution, and a recognition of its value."

The concept of "work-centered spirituality" is from the mind and heart of Pope John Paul II and it rings true in the hearts of workers because, from the beginning of time, women and men have experienced their God-like-ness through the use of their creative powers, their ability to make things different and better, their ability and desire to love and to heal.

Another great example of lay people making gospel happen in the marketplace is a pamphlet called *On the Firing Line*. The pamphlet is a position paper by the Business Executives for Economic Justice in Chicago. *On the Firing Line* is published by ACTA Publications in Chicago and should be read by every Christian manager—including bishops, priests and lay administrators in diocesan, school and parish positions.

This position paper tackles thorny questions related to the dismissal of employees. The pamphlet urges management to do everything possible to avoid firing or lay offs. When termination is inevitable, it is to be done in a way that protects the employees dignity and helps him or her find other employment.

The Business Executives for Economic Justice is a group of Chicago-area Catholic business and professional managers formed in response to the U.S. Catholic bishops' pastoral letter, *Economic Justice for All*. The group is a project of the National Center for the Laity in Chicago.

A final word, in this chapter, dealing with the growth of individual Christians as they live their role in the world.

Catholics are usually hesitant to speak openly about their personal spirituality and their relationship with God. I think that marketplace mission will demand a certain holy boldness on the part of the Catholic laity. While there is no need to imitate the extremes of over-eager fundamentalists, Catholics will find it necessary to become more comfortable and open in sharing their faith and understanding of the Word of God. There should be a contagious excitement about being a part of building up God's kingdom.

Good reading materials abound and at the end of this book I am offering a reading list and resources as a service to both individuals and groups of Catholics to confidently pursue their faith in the marketplace.

In speaking of Catholic evangelism, Father John Bertolucci, a great Catholic preacher, once said that too many Catholics were sacramentalized but not evangelized. In recent years, there has been a lot of emphasis on evangelization of Catholics, on developing a deeper relationship with Jesus and coming to grips with what it means to be a disciple of Jesus.

There have been many changes in both the Church and the world. Catholic spirituality has grown and developed over the years. We should not succumb to the temptation to disregard the past or to live in the past. Nor should we embrace change for change's sake or resist all change for sake of a false security.

In the next and final chapter, let's build a bridge between yesterday and today. Let's also look forward to tomorrow.

But first, our reflection.

REFLECTION

To all people of today I once again repeat the impassioned cry with which I began my pastoral ministry: "Do not be afraid! Open indeed, open wide the doors to Christ! Open to his saving power the confines of states and systems, political and economic, as well as the vast fields of culture, civilization and development. Do not be afraid! . . . Humanity is loved by God!" This very simple, yet profound proclamation is owed to humanity by the Church. Each Christian's words and life must make this proclamation resound: God loves you, Christ came for you, Christ is for you "the way, the truth and the life!" (Jn 14:6) (Christifideles Laici, op. cit., No.34)

Quiet Time

Am I tongue tied when it comes to telling people that Christ loves them and comes for them, that he is for them the way to true peace of mind and heart? When did I last tell someone about God's love?

Prayer

Lord Jesus, you told us not to worry about what we are to say when confronted with challenges to our faith or opportunities to share our faith. Help me Lord to develop a willing, eager, patient and compassionate attitude when sharing my faith in you. Amen.

Starter Questions

1. In the 1990s and beyond, there will be many opportunities to serve as a missionary for Christ in the world. What are some of the challenges I will face personally? What will we face together as Church? What gifts do I have to meet these particular challenges?

2. In what ways can I increase opportunities for sharing faith and my own mission agenda with fellow parishioners? Does the Marketplace Mission Group idea offer any practical possibility? What are other possibilities?

3. Do I see a need to grow in prayer, faith sharing, a sense of personal and community mission? How can this be achieved?

Commitment to Action

To further (my, our) mission in the marketplace, (I, we) will . . .

Prayer

Jesus, it's a little scary to make such a commitment. We can feel so inadequate, even when we work together. We are inadequate. But with you all things are possible. You promised to be with us always and to fill us with your powerful Spirit. We accept those promises now. Thank you, Jesus. Amen.

Chapter Five

A Bridge from Yesterday to Today

In January of 1990, we began "Re-Membering Church" in our parish of St. Mary Magdalen's, Altamonte Springs, Florida. "Re-Membering Church" is a program gaining recognition throughout the United States for outreach to alienated Catholics. It resembles the process of the Rite of Christian Initiation of Adults (RCIA) but deals more with reconciling Catholics with God and the Church and in healing the hurts that caused alienation in the first place.

An Important Lesson

Alienated Catholics, we have learned, leave the Church for a number of reasons. They feel hurt because of the way they were treated by some authority figure in the Church. They are divorced or divorced and remarried and are not aware of opportunities within the Church to work things out personally and spiritually. Some disagree with one or more of the official Church teachings. They were confused by the way in which changes were carried out following Vatican Council II. They feel they were not "being fed" in the Catholic Church and went to churches which they felt met their needs better.

In prison ministry and in speaking with neighbors and co-workers, I have heard many people say they left their churches because they considered them irrelevant to the challenges they had to face every day.

We can learn a good lesson if we reflect on the mistakes we all made in responding to the challenge of Vatican Council II.

That great council called first of all for a spiritual renewal, for a more active lay role in evangelization and in sanctifying the world through holiness and involvement, for a new and vibrant vision of Church which placed it in the middle of the world's tensions, problems and possibilities.

In too many cases, renewal never happened because we put the cart before the horse. Liturgical changes were made without adequate preparation and instruction, without the benefits of bringing the vision of the Council Fathers into the parish family and letting the parish family discover the wonders and power of that vision given by the Holy Spirit.

The scope of spiritual renewal mandated by the Council is only now, almost three decades later, beginning to take root. True, the liturgical changes, resisted so strongly by some and inaugurated so thoughtlessly by others, are one of the greatest signs of the spiritual dimension of the renewal called for by the Council Fathers. However, some Catholics are only now beginning to understand and appreciate these changes. Unfortunately, there are some people who are so resistant to change that they will never fully recognize the Lord speaking in and through the contemporary Church and the updated liturgy.

Again, in response to people who are leaving or have left the Catholic Church, we too often put the cart before the horse. We talk about sacraments, Church history, theology, liturgy and community before we offer them the fundamental invitation to conversion—to the way of Jesus, the truth of Jesus, the life of Jesus.

Here is an important consideration for our work in the marketplace. People do not really know the Church. If they are alienated Catholics, they see the Church through a film of anger and/or pain. If they are Protestants, they see the Church through their own traditions which broke away from the Catholic Church. If they are unchurched, they see the Church through the jaundiced eye of the secular press which fails to present the truth of what the Church is all about—and fails, too, in fairly reporting news about the Church. Also, too often when it comes to understanding the Church, many people are negatively influenced by the secular media which presents a gross caricature of what our Church is about.

A New Look at the Church

We have to give all these people a new look at the Church—the image the thousands saw on that first Pentecost after Jesus ascended into heaven.

On the first Pentecost, three thousand people converted to Jesus Christ. They did not say they were converting to Christianity or the Church. Those terms were not yet used. Peter and the other apostles were talking about the wonder of Jesus, the Son of God, the Messiah who died in our place, who rose from the dead and went to the Father and who will come again.

The Christian message begins with Jesus' death and resurrection, not with his birth in the Bethlehem stable. We have to realize that the gospels as we read them now are the product of a community reflecting on the meaning of Jesus Christ, his coming into the world, his teaching, dying and rising. The emphasis was not so much on the chronological order of his life story as on the meaning of his life, how he lived and what he did. Jesus *loved*, so he healed and taught and forgave sins. The big lesson is *love*. Jesus spoke of the kingdom of God. He said he was the Way, the Truth and the Life. He still is today and we are called to express the fullness of his healing love and power in our lives so others can come to know him.

For Peter and the other apostles, for the disciples and the three thousand converts on that first Pentecost, Jesus Christ, crucified, died and risen, *was* the message. This message is the core of our faith. This is what Christians are supposed to be excited about. It is Jesus to whom we call everyone and to whom we constantly turn and return after sinning.

The early Christians believed Jesus was coming again— real soon. They lived in community, selling their personal property and pooling their resources. No one would want; no one would be left out in the cold; no one would feel unloved or rejected.

Over the centuries, faith in Jesus Christ remained the core of Catholicism but it sometimes became submerged in rules, rubrics and regulations, in structure and symbols, in pieties and superficialities. Sometimes the faith flamed hotly and renewal swept through the Church. Sometimes certain saints became God's special instruments for renewal—Francis, for example.

In our own history, as Catholics in America, that faith in Jesus has become obscured and submerged in the culture and pressures of the times. Our way of being Catholic has preserved our faith and yet made it difficult for some to experience the faith and its mission fully.

Permit me an exaggeration for sake of emphasis. In the history of American Catholicism, Catholic lay people have for the most part been burdened with a second-class spirituality; Catholic laity were considered too ignorant to read Scripture without endangering their faith, too spiritually naive to grasp the height and breadth and depth of God's love; most Catholic lay people developed a strictly God-me relationship while, for security, they clung tightly to the tails of their pastors' cassocks; the sacraments were moments in which God came to them, unworthy as they might be, to forgive them and bring them closer to the possibilities of getting to heaven; the laity's role was one of supporting the Church and the apostolic mission of the hierarchy; the laity were expected to pray, pay and obey, as the old saying goes.

These conditions often made Catholics and their faith look pale alongside the more open, energetic and public style of other churches.

Along came Vatican council II, but not in a vacuum or as suddenly as most people tend to believe. When Pope John XXIII "opened the windows" of the Church to let in "fresh air," this saintly man had read the "signs of the times."

Throughout the world the laity had been on the move, motivated by their pastors who, in turn, had been motivated by the Catholic Action promoted by Pope Pius X. This saintly pope said the mission of the Church was to "restore all things in Christ," not only to lead "souls" to Christ. In his apostolic vision, the Church was supposed to lead all of civilization to Christ and help bring about a holy order in the world. As I understand it, Pius X began to recapture the vision of a missionary "people of God" (as Vatican Council II would put it) and he recognized the priesthood of the faithful, a spiritual power and mission flowing from the baptismal font, which directed and enabled them to bring the Gospel into the world (marketplace).

Still, in his vision, the laity served at the invitation of their bishops and pastors, had no real authority of their own and were not expected to initiate any movements without the express approval of ordained authority.

Catholic Action of Pius X

The Catholic Action of Pope Pius X was the apostolic vehicle to do what we today call evangelization. But, in his time, it was a work that stemmed from the mission of the hierarchy, not from the entire people of God. There were three principle characteristics of Catholic Action.

All are called, but not with the same urgency or in the same way. Each Catholic must respond according to his or her opportunities—and where there are no opportunities, the obligation ceases. This latter condition, I believe, gave rise to

many excuses not to share faith, e.g. "Well, I'm only a plumb-
er (or housewife or secretary or physician), not a priest or a
sister and I can't drop everything and go to Africa."

*Such apostolic work is the perfection and fullness of
Christianity*, in accordance with *Christ's will* as expressed in
the *Church's legislation*.

"Apostolic work" was primarily the work of the pope and
bishops. The Church's "law" proved that the mission was the
right mission and that the laity had the privilege to share in
the hierarchy's work. The emphasis was on Church authority
as expressed in Canon Law rather than on the more freeing
and inspiring Word of God.

*Catholic action does not cover the entire area of
apostleship*. Lay people do not share in the total mission of
the Church but only in those areas assigned by a bishop or
pastor—fund raising and teaching catechism, for example.
Lay people are primarily persons "needing" ministry, rather
than persons "sharing" ministry.

Our understanding of the mission of the people of God, in
and through Vatican Council II, builds on this vision of Pius
X. When John XXIII called the great Council, he was fully
aware of the movement begun by Catholic Action.
Throughout the world lay people were involved in spiritual
renewal and works of evangelization through Cursillo, Christian Family Movement, and various Third Orders promoted
by religious communities.

Catholic Action had lit a fire and the flame was now beginning to glow brightly in the Church. God's Spirit was speaking to his people through his people, and the saintly Pope
John, along with others, were hearing the voice of God.

A Renewed Understanding

Today, we understand that within the context of a hierar-
chical and apostolic Church, each Christian—through baptism, life experience and affirmation from the Church—

receives a calling, should have a personal attachment to Christ and has a personal destiny and dignity.

The calling comes from Christ. In all cases, from the domestic in a mansion to the pope, the call to be a Christian and to share in Christ's mission comes from Christ. The call is to ongoing conversion, to repentance, to holiness. Each of us faces, with Peter, the question: "And you, who do you say that I am?"

Each disciple must have a deep, personal attachment to Jesus Christ. To be a disciple means to be a follower. To "follow" in this sense means to turn away from the old ways, the old beliefs, the familiar crutches and to place total and complete faith in Jesus, to let his Way, be our way, his Truth our truth, his Life our life.

To be attached to Christ means to be detached from other things. This does not mean we cannot enjoy or own beautiful art, have good friends, truly love our spouses and children. It does mean that all things and everyone in life is appreciated and loved differently—with a freeing detachment. When we love as Jesus loves, we are not possessive and overbearing. Beauty is shared with everyone and those we love are set free and loved into holiness rather than possessed and smothered in emotional slavery.

As disciples, we each have a destiny and dignity. We don't believe in predestination, but when we truly "follow" Jesus we inherit the kingdom. That is our destiny *if* we truly follow Jesus. It's his promise. Our dignity as disciples comes from Jesus Christ himself. With St. Paul, each disciple can say, "It is not I who lives, but Christ lives in me." The converted and committed follower of Jesus shares the life of God and that indeed speaks of dignity and destiny.

Our new understanding of Church, mission and personal call to mission is both a blessing and an occasion for misunderstanding.

The wonder of a personal call from God is made all the more wonderful when it is heard and answered within the structure of the Church founded by Jesus. Through the

Church, and yes, through "obedience" to authentic authority in the Church, our call and response to the call are always tested, corrected, affirmed and strengthened. Nothing is more deadly to the mission of Christ's Church than well-meaning people who by-pass the Church in the name of Jesus who calls them into the Church!

To avoid that pitfall, however, does not mean we have to reject the new vision of Church.

In many parishes and dioceses throughout the world, Catholic laity are answering their call from Christ, are developing a deep attachment to Christ and are experiencing new dignity and realizing their Christian destiny within the structure of the Church. Their bishops and pastors have heard the call of the Spirit and are responding.

What do we do, you may ask, if we are unfortunate to have a bishop or a pastor who does not grasp this vision in the same way or seems to have no vision at all. That question has a simple answer, so simple it might seem simplistic. You do what you can when you can. You don't do anything to further alienate the bishop or pastor or turn people against them. You don't divide the community, but you work to build it up through love.

However, if we are truly prayerful and obedient, we will sometimes find it necessary to address certain issues. Some problems are so serious that it would be a failure to love if we let them continue to disturb the faith community. Confrontation must always be done in love, with a view to healing and wholeness in the community.

We sometimes unwittingly become one another's crosses. If we love one another, we can become like Simon of Cyrene and help one another carry those crosses. We can listen, try to understand, try to change where we need to change.

The bottom line is this. If you are not praying for that pastor or those parishioners, if you are not dying to self for him or them, then you yourself are failing to love. When necessary, you must be willing to lay down your life (your personal preferences and vision) for the sake of the others.

It is hard to understand but the proof is in the dying and rising of Jesus. It is in dying (failing to achieve what we know is God's vision) for others (loving those who hinder us and even Jesus himself) that we are born to eternal life (which begins in this life with the dying to self and rising in Christ's love).

The mission is first of all to love. Not to win arguments or even to convert souls. There can be no Christian victory apart from sacrificial love; there can be no conversion to Christ without genuine, unconditional sacrificial love.

If any one says, 'My love is fixed on God,' yet hates his brother, he is a liar. One who has no love for the brother he has seen cannot love the God he has not seen. (1Jn 4:20)

To make Marketplace Mission a top priority will demand a deep spiritual renewal of personal and community relationships.

We have to be sure, as Christians and as a parish, that we know the meaning of love and that we practice love. Without love as the foundation of our ministries, we can never hope to live up to the demands of evangelization and service in the modern world.

Making Marketplace Miracles Happen

How can the typical parish bring about personal and community renewal and dedication to Marketplace Mission?

Some parishes have very successful parish retreats. These differ from the typical mission where people come to the parish church each evening for a week to hear an outside speaker. The parish retreat often is led by parishioners themselves, working with the pastor and parish staff to discern the needs of the community.

The retreat can be held over a weekend at a retreat center or even in the parish hall with people going home evenings. Baby-sitting, in any case, should be provided so parents of small children can benefit fully from the retreat.

The content of the retreat has to be determined by the parish itself, with pastor, staff and parishioners active in the planning process.

With a view to Marketplace Mission, however, I would suggest that such a weekend retreat encompass traditional, personal "spirituality" involving prayer and sacraments as well as concern for social justice and other contemporary issues. Also, the retreat should be rooted in both Tradition and Scripture. Above all, the retreat team should remember that the focus is on the marketplace, not on the parish as an institution or community and not on parish needs. One objective for the retreat is to help lay people recognize how they are potential miracles in the marketplace.

I have turned 360° from my former position that "praying" is not necessary if "your whole life is a prayer." Some 20 years after I made that foolish statement in *Ragin' Cajun* I have come to realize that if we are not "praying," there is precious little chance our lives will be a prayer.

Such a retreat, after prayerful deliberation, may look something like this.

MARKETPLACE MISSION RETREAT

FRIDAY EVENING — Church with Pastor and facilitator presiding

Opening prayer service (welcome, scripture reading, homily and light service using the Paschal candle)

— Parish Hall

"Building on Yesterday" Orientation by facilitator—a brief review of the development of lay ministry/spirituality

Talk on personal spirituality and prayer by a parishioner—reflective and experiential

Social time

SATURDAY MORNING — Parish Hall

Mass

Continental breakfast

"Who are We as Church?" Facilitator speaks on stages of conversion, models of church and relationship with the world

Break

"What this Parish Means to Me" Talk by a local parishioner

Break for silent reflection

"Digesting the Meal" Audience reactions and questions to presentations

Midday prayer

Lunch

SATURDAY AFTERNOON — Parish Hall

Talk by facilitator centered on Henry Libersat's *Miracle in the Marketplace: Healing and Loving in the Modern World*
a) Daily life and work as Church work
b) Embracing the world instead of fleeing it
c) Seeing the world as part of the kingdom
d) Loving people where they are and being ready to share the love of Christ and the Catholic faith

Break

"My Mission in the World" Three 15 minute talks by parishioners: policeman, judge or attorney; teacher, nurse or secretary; personnel manager, estate planner or banker

Group discussion

Dinner

SATURDAY EVENING — Parish Hall

"Applying the Principles" Small group brainstorming discussions on Marketplace Missions
a) mutual support in the workplace
b) witnessing in the marketplace
c) Record results on newsprint and tape to wall

Night prayer

Social

SUNDAY MORNING — Parish Hall

Morning prayer   ·

Continental breakfast

"Sharing the Vision" Small groups report to the large group with open, brief discussion on each report

Break

"Opportunities, Challenges, Responses" Talk by facilitator giving an overview of the challenges in today's society, the global spirituality needed to respond, examples of how people are responding all over the world. Handout of resources, books and organizations for ongoing formation

Mass-scheduled parish Mass

Lunch

"Where do we go from here?" Small group discussions on the following topics:
a) How can our parish incorporate this new focus on lay ministry to help everyone understand his/her role in Marketplace Mission?
b) How will each individual be supported in his/her Marketplace Mission?
c) How do we form Marketplace Mission Groups? How often and where will they meet? How will they be part of

the overall parish mission and ministry?

"Toward a Parish Marketplace Mission" All gather for small group reports to adopt a plan, set timelines and deadlines, select a coordinator, decide how groups will be formed, schedule follow-up meetings to keep momentum going.

"Go Out Into the World" closing ceremony in which the Pastor commissions laity as Marketplace Missionaries

PARISH FOLLOW UP

The parish may follow up the retreat by a bulletin insert announcing a Marketplace Mission Sunday. On that day, homilies would be geared toward helping lay people understand the Vatican II concept of lay spirituality and John Paul's spirituality of work.

The thrust from the pulpit should be ongoing, using frequent examples of lay mission in the marketplace.

Marketplace Mission should be central to parish life, not just another program. Through Marketplace Mission, the entire parish can become more conscious of its obligation to "Go out into the world."

This suggested retreat is only one idea of how a parish might begin to expand the laity's role in the marketplace. Surely there are many other ideas.

It is time, now for our final reflection. You will find, after the reflection, a list of suggested readings.

But before you go on, a final word.

The Father and the Lord Jesus send the Holy Spirit upon us. The Spirit gives us wisdom, discernment, faith, hope and strength. Our only limitations are those we place upon ourselves.

I want to urge all who read this book to look and listen carefully in their world; look and listen for the Lord.

Hear a co-worker complaining about working conditions or a child who is hooked on drugs; see a beggar on the street and the policeman directing traffic, the sanitation workers cleaning the city streets and the farmer planting seeds; see children walking to school and men and women running into combat. Hear the cries of the poor, the hungry, the children whose bloated bellies are common in the Third World and in American slums; hear the silent screams of young runaway teenagers, boys and girls, forced into prostitution, the cries of women kidnapped and sold as sex slaves in Japan. See the homeless walking our streets, sleeping in rags and trying to stay warm under soggy newspaper. Hear the pleas of people trying to get help for this or that group of needy. See with un-prejudiced eyes business leaders trying to create more jobs for the unemployed; see gangs guzzling booze outside the local bar.

Look and see. Listen and hear.

And when you see and hear any or all of these things, turn quickly to your five loaves and two fish. Listen and hear with faith that jarring challenge: "You give them to eat."

You can make the miracle happen—because **you are the miracle in the marketplace!**

REFLECTION

Then the just will ask him: 'Lord, when did we see you hungry and feed you or thirsty and give you drink? When did we welcome you away from home or clothe you in our nakedness? When did we visit you when you were ill or in prison?' The king will answer them 'I assure you as often as you did it for one of my least brothers, you did it for me.' (Mt 25:37-40)

Quiet Time

Have I felt a call from the Spirit to renew myself in love and service? Do I hear the cry of the poor? Do I recognize anyone in need as "poor?" Am I aware of the different kinds of prisons in which Jesus' sisters and brothers suffer—loneliness, emotional distress, ignorance, habitual sin?

Am I a true *follower* of Jesus? Do I believe *in* him or just acknowledge that he exists?

In my relationships with my parish community, am I loving and helpful, or cool and distant?

Prayer

Lord, I realize that I am an individual Christian with individual responsibilities—but I am also part of the Church, of my parish community. I need my brothers and sisters, Lord, so give me the grace to remember to seek them out to share my faith and my hopes and my plans. Jesus, help me help my parish to be a true missionary force in today's world. Amen.

Starter questions

1. Am I (are we) ready to begin in earnest to make the marketplace our mission?

2. What are the most pressing social and personal needs I encounter in my community, friends and co-workers everyday? What are the marketplace needs my fellow parishioners, pastor and parish staff are discovering?

3. What can (I, we) do to face the challenge and call of Jesus to care for the people in our lives?

4. How might (I, we) begin?

Commitment to Action

To further a parish-based approach to lay mission in the marketplace, (I, we) will . . .

Prayer

Lord, Father. Your kingdom come. May your will be done in us and through us. Give us your Spirit. Help us to be your eyes, ears, heart. Let us love as you love. Give us a constant awareness of the example and love of your Son, Jesus. Help us to be like him. Mary, our Mother, intercede for us. Ask Jesus and the Father to make us one through the power and love of the Spirit. Amen.

Suggested Reading and Resources

Droel, William L., and Pierce, Gregory F. Augustine. *Confident and Competent, A Challenge for the Lay Church*, ACTA Publications.

Ghezzi, Bert. *Becoming More Like Jesus*, Our Sunday Visitor Press. *Keeping Your Kids Catholic*, Servant Publications.

Green, Thomas H., S.J. *Opening to Prayer, When the Well Runs Dry, Darkness in the Marketplace*, Ave Maria Press.

Haughey, John C., S.J. *Converting 9 to 5, A Spirituality of Daily Work*, Crossroad Publications. *The Holy Use of Money, Personal Finance in the Light of Christian Faith*, Crossroad Publications.

Pope John Paul II, *Christifideles Laici, Redemptor Hominis, The Apostolic Exhortation on Family*, and *Laborem Exercens* — all available from *Origins*, Catholic News Service, 3211 4th St. N.E., Washington, D.C. 10017-1194.

Knight, David, *His Word*, St. Anthony Messenger Press.

Leege, David C., "Catholics and the Civic Order: Parish Participation, Politics and Civic Participation," *Notre Dame Study of Catholic Parish Life*, University of Notre Dame.

Libersat, Henry. *Way, Truth and Life*, and *Do Whatever He Tells You*, Daughters of St. Paul. *Caught in the Middle*, Crossroad Publications.

McKenna, Briege with Henry Libersat. *Miracles Do Happen*, Servant Publications.

Ortiz, Juan Carlos with Jamie Buckingham. *Call to Discipleship*, Logos International.

National Conference of Catholic Bishops, *The Challenge of*

86

Peace: God's Promise and Our Response, Economic Justice for All: Catholic Social Teaching and the U.S. Economy, both available from *Origins*, see above.

National Center for the Laity, series of monographs on "The Spirituality of Work," 1 E. Superior St. No. 311, Chicago, IL 60611.

Resources

Catholic Business Guild, St. Peter Parish, 507 South Tryon Street, Charlotte, NC 18101.

St. Boniface Parish, 8330 Johnson Street, Pembroke Pines, FL 33024.

National Center for the Laity, 1 E. Superior St. No. 311, Chicago, IL 60611

Gratitude to . . .

Resurrection Press for asking me to do this little book on a subject of great importance in the contemporary Church

Gregory Augustine Pierce of the National Center for the Laity, Chicago; Father Robert McGuire, S.J., advisor to Resurrection Press, and Father Ray Larsen, Diocese of Orlando, for reading and responding to this manuscript with valuable suggestions

Father John C. Haughey, S.J., founder of The Catholic Business Guild, for writing the foreword

Emilie Teutschman, Acquisitions Editor of Resurrection Press, for excellent editing and direction

My parish family of St. Mary Magdalen, Altamonte Springs, Florida, for giving me a home in which faith is alive and effective, especially to Chuck Lorenz, Frank Daly, George Meyer and Doug Huth for sharing their marketplace mission with me

Those people whose names appear in this book—for their information, help and encouragement, and, last but not least, Lady Margaret, my wife, whose patience, love, encouragement, prayers and insights level the mountains and fill the valleys.

Other Resurrection Press
Publications and Audiocassettes

Of Life and Love. Fr. Jim Lisante. Foreword by John
Powell. Preface by Archbishop Roger Mahony. $4.95

Award-winning columnist Fr. Jim Lisante offers his words of
wisdom and encouragement in his first full-length book.
Whatever your age, wherever you are in life, Fr. Jim's timely
writings on Family Matters and Respect Life issues will challenge and inspire you.

"Excellent spiritual reading for parents, teens and teachers."
Praying

Transformed by Love. The Way of Mary Magdalen.
Sr. Margaret Magdalen, csmv. Foreword by Jean Vanier.

Drawing from Mary Magdalen's experience, the author shows
the vital role of transformed passion as a God-given and essential part of the Christian life. Each chapter is based on an
aspect of Mary's transformation through love, but widens out
to embrace life experiences that touch us all: passion, peni-
tence, fervor, darkness in prayer, freedom. $5.95

**Give Them Shelter. Responding to Hunger and Home-
lessness**. Michael Moran.

The amazing story of the Interfaith Nutrition Network's soup
kitchens and emergency shelters, the network of volunteers
and donations which maintain The INN, and the breakdown
of the underlying causes of hunger and homelessness. Written
with wisdom, humor and compassion by the Director of The
INN. $5.95

Behold the Man. Seven Meditations on the Passion, Death and Resurrection of Jesus. Judy Marley, S.F.O.

These meditations on the mental suffering of Jesus during his last days on earth take us on a journey from the poignant fellowship of the Last Supper to Golgotha, and beyond that to resurrection triumph. A passport to an unforgettable journey with Jesus. $2.95

RVC Liturgical Series

Brief, easy-to-read books for those actively involved in liturgical ministry or who simply wish better to understand the Catholic liturgy.

Our Liturgy: Your Guide to the Basics. Describes and discusses the varieties of Liturgical Ministry and clearly explains Liturgical Objectives and Order of Mass. $4.25

The Great Seasons: Your Guide to Celebrating. Offers valuable insights to help with parish liturgy planning and to deepen private celebration of Advent, the Christmas Season, Lent, the Triduum and Easter Season. $3.25

The Liturgy of the Hours: Your Guide to Praying. An informative introduction to praying the Divine Office, with practical suggestions for parish implementation. $3.95

The Lector's Ministry: Your Guide to Proclaiming the Word. Not only gives practical advice but also discusses the Scripture-rooted spirituality required of a lector. $3.25

Our Spirit-Life Collection of Audiocassettes

Our *Spirit Life Collection* of audiocassettes brings you the most up-to-date information on religious, ethical and moral issues. Listening at home or in the car—alone or in a group—will uplift, educate and challenge you to walk the walk of committed discipleship.

Praying on Your Feet: A Contemporary Spirituality for Active Christians. Fr. Robert Lauder.
45 min. $5.95

Have you ever felt guilty about being too busy to pray? Fr. Lauder assures us that spirituality in today's world can be achieved on our feet as well as on our knees.

Annulment: Healing-Hope-New Life.
Msgr. Thomas Molloy.
60 min. $5.95

In lay language Msgr. Molloy unravels the myth and mystery surrounding the annulment process. "A healing process, a time for meaningful reflection, growth and new beginnings."

Divided Loyalties: Church Renewal Through a Reformed Priesthood. Anthony T. Padovano, Ph.D S.T.D.
60 min. $6.95

In this thought-provoking and timely reflection on today's Church, Dr. Padovano exhorts us to fashion a new Church. His keen historical perspectives, powerful analogies and loving example of service will inspire you to make the Church a credible Church where hope, truth and mercy prevail.